# Let Me Tell You, Let Me Sing!

collected poems

# Let Me Tell You, Let Me Sing!

collected poems by

Kathie Giorgio

© 2025 Kathie Giorgio. All rights reserved.
This material may not be reproduced in any form, published,
reprinted, recorded, performed, broadcast,
rewritten, or redistributed without
the explicit permission of Kathie Giorgio.
All such actions are strictly prohibited by law.

Cover design by Shay Culligan
Cover art by Ron Wimmer, Wimmer Photography
Author photo by Ron Wimmer, Wimmer Photography

ISBN: 978-1-63980-987-5

Kelsay Books
502 South 1040 East, A-119
American Fork, Utah 84003
Kelsaybooks.com

This collection is dedicated to my high school
creative writing teacher, Duane Stein.
I am now about three times older than he was when he taught me.
We are still good friends.

At the end of our poetry unit, he told me to stick with fiction.
I listened to him, and went on to my career as a novelist
and short story writer. But poetry wouldn't leave me alone,
and for many years, I wrote it in secret.

And now . . . this is my fifth book of poetry.

So this is dedicated to you, Duane. I love you,
and I'm so grateful to you.
But sometimes . . . you were WRONG!

# Acknowledgments

The following poems from this collection have been previously published. They are listed in the order they appear in the book:

*Blue Heron Review:* "Retreat," "Savor"
*Dash:* "Depends on the Day"
*Don't Let Me Keep You:* "Age Old," "Teething," "House at Night," "Baby Blue," "The One That Got Away," "Daughters," "Always"
*Enlarged Hearts:* "God, Adam, Eve, and Woman"
*Jade Ring Anthology:* "Again," first place in poetry, 2021 Wisconsin Writers Association Jade Ring Contest
*No Matter Which Way You Look, There Is More to See:* "Easing The Words," "By and By"
*Persimmon Tree:* "The House on Pine Street"
*Poetry Leaves Anthology:* "Harvest Moon," presented in the Poetry Leaves exhibit in Waterford, Michigan
*Raven's Perch:* "She Listens"
*Rockvale Review:* "Copper Moon," "Orange Moon," "Black Sky"
*Rosebud:* "The Passing of Time and Little Known Facts," "Light," honorable mention in Rosebud magazine's poetry contest
*The Voices Project:* "Social Distance"
*Wisconsin Fellowship of Poets 2025 Desk Calendar:* "Predawn Dreaming"

# Other Books by Kathie Giorgio

Poetry Collections
- *Olivia in Five, Seven, Five: Autism in Haiku* (Finishing Line Press, 2022)
- *No Matter Which Way You Look, There Is More to See* (Finishing Line Press, 2020)
- *When You Finally Said No* (Finishing Line Press, 2019)
- *True Light Falls in Many Forms* (The Main Street Rag Publishing Company, 2016)

Novels
- *Don't Let Me Keep You* (Black Rose Writing, 2024)
- *Hope Always Rises* (Black Rose Writing, 2023)
- *All Told* (Austin Macauley Publishers, 2022)
- *If You Tame Me* (Black Rose Writing, 2019)
- *In Grace's Time* (Black Rose Writing, 2017)
- *Rise from the River* (The Main Street Rag Publishing Company, 2015)
- *Learning to Tell (a Life)Time* (The Main Street Rag Publishing Company, 2013)
- *The Home for Wayward Clocks* (The Main Street Rag Publishing Company, 2011)

Short Story Collections
- *Oddities & Endings: The Collected Stories of Kathie Giorgio* (The Main Street Rag Publishing Company, 2016)
- *Enlarged Hearts* (The Main Street Rag Publishing Company, 2012)

Essay Collection
- *Today's Moment of Happiness Despite the News: A Year of Spontaneous Essays* (Black Rose Writing, 2018)

# Contents

**PART ONE**     Family, Here and Gone, But Forever Held

| | |
|---|---|
| Age-Old | 17 |
| Teething | 18 |
| House at Night | 19 |
| Baby Blue | 20 |
| The One That Got Away | 21 |
| When Quiet Descends | 22 |
| On the Day You See the Whale | 23 |
| She Listens | 24 |
| Light | 25 |
| One Foot Here, One Foot There | 26 |
| Daughters | 28 |
| Motherhood | 29 |
| Always | 30 |
| The Passing of Time and Little Known Facts | 31 |
| The House on Pine Street | 33 |
| History of Beds | 35 |
| Savor | 37 |
| Passing On | 39 |

**PART TWO**     The Sun, the Moon, and an Old Orange Cat

| | |
|---|---|
| Copper Moon | 43 |
| Orange Moon | 44 |
| Black Sky | 45 |
| Harvest Moon | 46 |
| Moonglow | 47 |
| Predawn Dreaming | 48 |
| Eclipse | 49 |
| Old Orange Cat | 50 |

PART THREE   When Poetry Tells a Story: Conflict, Climax, Resolution

| | |
|---|---|
| Easing the Words | 53 |
| One of Those Drives | 54 |
| Re: F | 55 |
| Depends on the Day | 56 |
| Again | 57 |
| Essential | 58 |
| Social Distance | 60 |
| When a City Screams | 62 |
| At the Registration Desk at the Y | 64 |
| Rhymes | 65 |
| Fall | 66 |
| Reality Calling | 67 |
| By and By | 68 |
| Missing on CraigsList's Missed Connections | 69 |
| My Place | 70 |
| When a Man Turns a Cartwheel | 71 |
| The Truth About Cows | 72 |
| Retreat | 74 |
| God, Adam, Eve, and Woman | 75 |

# PART ONE

## Family,
## Here and Gone,
## But Forever Held

# Age-Old

*haiku*

This baby, so new, her
skin pink with no age, glowing
with passed-down wisdom.

# Teething

*haiku*

Pearl white teeth erupt
bright signs of a peaceful soul
amid gums red with rage

# House at Night

*haiku*

Children sleep, dreams rise
fill the house with clouds of sighs
soft breath, soft sound, peace.

# Baby Blue

*haiku*

Baby bathed in blue.
Breath lost on a sunny day.
Sleep in peace, my son.

# The One That Got Away

*prose poem*

I've always heard you regret the one that got away. In fishing. In hunting. The ball that slides through ready hands. The lover who stays a night and then disappears in the morning. The thought that seems so important, but then fades into a gray mass of letters that don't say anything at all. The child. The baby! You fell into a dream that I couldn't share. A dream that only a three-week old could have, and a dream that you chose to follow. In my own dreams, I see you crawling onto a cloud. A cloud rimmed with blue. And a cloud that offers the temptation to fly, to soar, to be a part of a bigger blue, the biggest blue of all. Baby blue. The sky is just for you. I look up in the sky and I see you sometimes. You never laughed, but I hear your laugh. You never sang, but I hear you sing. You never said my name, but I hear you call me. Mama! I hear your cry and it makes me ache. I see your eyes when you look for me, but then you look away. To the sky. The sky is just for you. The sky is baby blue. It holds all the hearts and souls of those who are missed, who are regretted, the ones who got away, the ones that learned about Heaven before they knew about Earth. Yearned for Heaven. The way I yearn for you. Baby blue.

# When Quiet Descends

My daughter is away at orchestra camp,
doing whatever it is you do at orchestra camp.
And it's a new kind of quiet here tonight.
The house is usually quiet, as she is in that phase
of the closed bedroom door and headphones
(though I can still hear her sing and I treasure that brave voice).
It's quiet and quieter, not even the sound of:
her door opening
her socked feet coming down the hall
the fetching of water in the kitchen
And sometimes, oh, sometimes, the swish of her spin as she says
in that brave voice,
"Mama!"
and curls her 15-year-old self into my lap,
her long, lean body into my lap
and she is five again.
A few moments of talk and then she kisses my cheek
before sock-footing to her bedroom:
Closed door.
Brave voice.
Singing.
It's quieter here tonight.
Quiet upon quiet.
And I feel the lack of her.
I miss her.
And that missing ripple-ponds out to missing the first three,
my boy, my boy, my girl,
who left my lap long ago.
This one, this one, is my last.
I hear the quiet upon quiet of my future.

# On the Day You See the Whale

On the day you see
the whale
its broad back arched
and sparkling in the sun
like a wave of the same sea
that never rests,
you also hear your teen daughter's voice
as she speaks to her boyfriend
on an iPad that lets her see
his face shine in Wisconsin
while you and she are playing
by the ocean in Oregon.
And her face shines to him.
And you think how these
are miracles.
The whale.
Her face.
The sparkles.

## She Listens

My daughter's new boyfriend invites her
to a gun show.
Five days after
a mob storms the Capitol Building
wielding Confederate flags, hate banners,
weapons and slurs and profanity,
cheers that bring chills to the bone,
My daughter is twenty years old.

I can't shelter her from the news
from headlines, articles
rants on Facebook and Twitter
video of a police officer being beaten
to death
by an American flag.
Can I keep her from an arena
with table after table of guns?
And a boy who will pick one up,
feel the weight in his palm,
maybe hold it outstretched to
sight down the length of a barrel.
Imagine squeezing the trigger.
Picture his prey.

I say no.
Just in case.

She listens.
Smiles.
Says she already told him
No.

# Light

*prose poem*

So you walk with your daughter and there's the glow of fireflies and streetlight and starlight and moonlight and the bright white of paper against the cobbles and you pick it up and read *Will You Go to Heaven When You Die?* and you pitch it away just like you've been burned because you don't think you'll ever see that Light or maybe you have but it's not the light that's expected because sometimes the light's from within   Quiet   You walk for the hour that the dark really falls and it drapes on your shoulders not like a shroud but like Earth's sigh on your skin   It's summer   You hear the quack of a duck and the peep of its babe and the throb of the frogs and the song of the cricket and loud splashes that scare you because there just might be gators (your daughter) or muskrats (you)   There's the soft language of walkers and the smiles of strangers and one of them God-blesses you and because you're polite you say thank you and who knows?   it might help   And your laughter floats up like fireflies and streetlight and starlight and moonlight   This lit dark is a sigh you wear home.

# One Foot Here, One Foot There

On the front porch, there is a box
addressed to my 22-year-old daughter.
She rips into it, thrilled as any child who
receives mail which is only for her.
Inside, there is a plush red teddy bear.
It has little black horns and a red arrowed tail.
A devil.
She hugs it and says, "I bought it for myself."
She carries it to her room, still her room,
even though she's been gone almost 4 years
to college. She graduates in May.
She's been buying many stuffed animals lately.
Mostly things called Squishmallows.
Square or oval puffy shapes with faces meant to be
cats, dogs, lizards, cows, octopi, horses, and even
cups of tea, coffee, soda, milk, hunks of cheese,
a hamburger.
She displays them in her dorm room
and in her bedroom, here at home.
She's 22. A college senior. Bound for grad school.
I look at her, hugging the red devil bear,
talking to it in a soft voice I've known all her life.
And I see her with one foot planted in a safe childhood
and the other foot planted in a promising, but uncertain
adulthood.
Just like I hold her tightly to me, every night when she's home,
and tell her I'll see her in the morning,

or send a text message when she's at school, the screen
bubbling with red hearts, my own heart bubbling too
as I turn her to face away from me
to step directly into the future.
She hugs the bear.
I hug her.
We let go.

# Daughters

*haiku*

When daughters leave home,
the little girls stay behind,
peeking from corners.

# Motherhood

When a mother hugs her daughter,
she feels the world on those young shoulders.
The weight from riding on two wheels
to driving on four with friends in the car
From the very first tampon
to choices in birth control
From figuring out kissing
to could I be pregnant
From will I be accepted
to am I going to flunk out
From do I really like him
to should I get married
From am I ready for a baby
to why is she crying like that
From am I good at my job
to should I be home with my kids
From should I forgive him
to can I be alone
From moving away
to coming home
A mother feels this world
when she hugs her daughter
and she takes some of it, most of it,
as much as will be allowed
as her own.
Adds it to her own question.
Was I a good mother?
Am I a good mother?
Still?
She looks for answers for them both.

# Always

*haiku*

Mothers watch silent
from the shadows of the past.
Their eyes gleam with love.

# The Passing of Time and Little Known Facts

*prose poem*

That moment.
That moment when you are at the zoo, pushing a stroller. But unlike all the strollers before, including a double-stroller, this one doesn't have your own child in it. It has your granddaughter and she's three and she's telling you facts about tigers you never knew. They can be blue. They go to museums. And they like to eat Taco Bell. She pronounces it, "TYE-grrr." In front of you walks your almost–16-year-old daughter, hand in hand with Boyfriend #2. Their heads are close together. You remember when she used to tell you facts you never knew. You remember a little orange rubber tyrannosaurus rex named Baby Dino who fit in the palm of her hand and went everywhere tucked in her fingers. Now Baby Dino is tucked away in your dresser drawer. He is missing his arms and one back leg. Beside you, your 29-year-old daughter tells you about the classes she's teaching, the work she's doing, the list of mathematicians she posted on Facebook, one for every letter of the alphabet. A future wedding. A busy life. She sees giraffes and lights up and you remember how the never-known facts she told you were about giraffes. You remember a series of pink ragdolls she slept with from the time she was two weeks old. You bought more in secret for when one would wear out. In your storage unit, you have a box of over 20 pink ragdolls. Their name was Pinky. When you buy your granddaughter a pink TYE-grrr, she names her Pinky, and your daughter says, "Well, that's imaginative." You smile. On your other side, your 30-year-old son. He speaks of work, insurance, a new car. His attention is drawn by the old painted dinosaur tracks on the ground, left over from when dinosaurs invaded the zoo and he was four and had no interest in the live animals, he needed to get to the dinosaurs, like your granddaughter needs to get to the TYE-grrrs now. He told you all

the never-known facts about dinosaurs. His were accurate. You remember a blue dinosaur that snored when it rocked in your son's tiny arms. His name was Dynomite. You don't have him tucked away—he is at your son's apartment. But you know where he is.

That moment. The rush of time in your ears, the ache of time in your bones, the passing of it right before your eyes.

# The House on Pine Street

My kids send me photos of their father
tearing apart the house of their childhood.
The house he and I bought together in 1987.
The house I left behind in 1997
with him in it.
The children are grown and in homes of their own.
Despite twenty-five years gone, I still somehow consider
that house mine.
I still feel Me in it. I still feel my kids.
My ex rips out the cabinets.
He rips out the counters and the floor.
He tears out the island where I used to sit every day
for breakfast
for lunch
a phone to my ear at noon on a routine call to my mother
who is no longer alive.
He rips out the pantry. On the door, there used to be
a huge calendar, to track all of the kids' activities
and my own. Track our lives together.
He rips out the half wall between the kitchen and the living room
that half wall where I used to lean and tell him about my day
while I kept an eye on the dinner, bubbling on the stove
and the kids did their homework in their rooms.
The house, my kids say, is going to look completely different.
And I see in their eyes the Christmas stockings that hung
from the half wall
the snacks grabbed from the pantry.
Those snacks shared after school and before bed,
all three of them laughing at the kitchen table.
And I feel, as he tears apart the kitchen, that he
tears out the last vestiges of Me. Of those kids. In that house.

Who I was
in that house.
Who they were.
1532 Pine Street.
With the memories in my eyes,
reflected in my kids' eyes,
I hug all three
and tell them again their stories.

# History of Beds

When you're born, you're put in a cage
a mattress surrounded by bars.
And you cry.
But then you grow older and your bed
grows with you
toddler to twin
you have sheets with rainbows and unicorns
and a bedspread filled with pink ruffles.
When you are fifteen, you have a boy to your room
and your bed becomes a rumple of new smells and
touches and suddenly, you don't want rainbows anymore.
But how can you tell your mother?
"I'm too old," you say.
And you are. She knows.
Soon you move out and your bed grows double and you
cover it with the richness of a quilt and underneath
silk sheets. Bright colors. Solids.
As time moves past, your bed grows to a queen and then
a king. King of the castle, and you want one,
so you add a husband. Who rumples the sheets with
smells and touches that are no longer
unfamiliar.
And you look to the bed at different times during the day,
there is meaning there, a secret, something hidden under
the covers besides the silk sheets.
Until they become flannel.
Children jump in during early morning hours on Saturday
when you are supposed to be able to sleep,
but you don't mind, because your children
smell like their night-before baths and you smile at
your husband with your own night-before and you
know what will come again on Saturday night.

And then the children are gone.
And then the husband is gone.
You sell the king bed.
You bring back a double.
And you sleep alone now. Your bed is
the comfort of memories.
You return to cotton and ruffles.
When you die, it is in a bed that isn't yours
but has rails
It's a mattress surrounded by bars.
And you cry.

# Savor

I've become
the grandma with the candy dish
It sits on my piano
a white ceramic pumpkin with
Give Thanks in gold scroll
and inside, jewels of hard candy
root beer barrels
cinnamon disks
pink and white peppermint
green and white spearmint
butterscotch
and sometimes, sometimes
licorice squares
My Nana had a crystal candy bowl
on some furniture she called a buffet
My mother said to never take any
It's been there for years and years, she said
Don't touch!
I snuck some anyway And while the
cellophane stuck to the candy, it still
tasted good
My Grandma's candy dish was her purse.
She kept Halls Mentholyptus cough drops in there
which I begged for and ate like candy
They were the originals, square, in a wrapper like
lifesavers
They tasted like Vicks Mentholatum Rub, which she put
under my nose every night, and just a bit on my tongue,
when we shared a bedroom
until she died
I still always choose Halls Mentholyptus, and I put

Vicks in my nostrils every night
Now
I keep jewels in my candy dish on my piano
and tell my granddaughter to take not one, but
a handful
choose all the flavors
Savor.
They're from me.

# Passing On

When my adult son loses his cat,
an old blind orange longhair who dies in his sleep
after a tumble down the basement stairs,
I hear my boy cry as he did
when he was teased and bullied at school
when he thought Good Friday meant we were
all going to die and rise to Heaven and
he didn't want to die or go to Heaven
just yet,
when I asked him to sing to me the song he
learned in preschool and he didn't want to
and I threatened to never let him go back to
school again because I was paying for him to sing
and he needed to sing to me. His mother.
I was a young mother, just 23 when I gave birth
to a boy only six pounds heavy, and who felt like
a swaddled football in my arms.
"He's heavy," I said, never having held a newborn before,
"He's not," said the nurse.
His first cries made me so scared.
There was so much I didn't know.
Now he is 37 years old and I still hear the little boy
when he cries.
And I am still afraid.
But I hear my echo in his voice when he comforts my
8-year-old granddaughter
who cries over losing the cat who was the firstborn
in her house
and she's never known a day without him.
My son talks softly to her
I hear
And I am no longer afraid.

# PART TWO

## The Sun,
## the Moon,
## and an Old Orange Cat

# Copper Moon

*haiku*

copper moon tonight
penny among silver stars
treasure in the sky

# Orange Moon

*haiku*

Orange moon, shine down,
blind the chaos we live in
with soft moonlit peace.

# Black Sky

*haiku*

On a moonless night
the sky wears black in mourning
the stars shimmer tears

# Harvest Moon

*haiku*

The moon at half mast
glows silver dreams and gold truths
as sighs twirl the earth

# Moonglow

*haiku*

my eyes see the moon
but it's my soul that glows bright
silver reflection.

# Predawn Dreaming

daydreaming when the day is still dark
ephemeral ethereal unrefined undefined
moonlit hope
starlit peace

# Eclipse

*(April 8, 2024)*

On the day of the eclipse
my hibiscus blooms
bright orange sunshine flower
bringing light even in moments
of long-lasting shadow.

# Old Orange Cat

*(In memory of Edgar Allen Paw)*

*haiku*

Old orange cat curls
his tail around his life and
purrs warm wise rhythm.

PART THREE

When Poetry Tells
a Story:

Conflict,
Climax,
Resolution

# Easing the Words

When the warm stone is pressed into my palm
my fingers close around it and every knuckle cracks.
Amazing, the muscles used in writing.
Shoulders hunched at the keyboard
Hands striking, restriking, remarking, refining
Words on a screen for a page someplace else.
For someone else.

Warm stones eased on shoulders, pressed down to a stretch.
Tendons and joints release storylines
Grow supple for new plots and turns.

Warm stones on the ears, pull the lobes, press behind
Empty the voices and the voices and the voices
Protagonists
Antagonists
And the secondaries, especially that one, who
strides to the front of the brain and insists he's not
secondary and lopes off into a story of his own, before the
last is finished and so suddenly, there are two storypaths
twisting in my brain, two trains of thought, two begging to be
done and up front and alone.
Stones on the ears, tugs and stretches
Make room for the new voices just waiting.

Warm stones on the temples and then placed on the eyes and
turn to salty river rocks as tears stream down my cheeks.
There is no story, after all, without conflict.

# One of Those Drives

*prose poem*

It was one of those drives. One of those drives where your husband turns to you and says, "I used to go to Bennigan's with Mary Ann and Weird April." All blue above, green beyond rich below. "Weird April said once, I'm going to order the fucking chicken wings to floss my teeth." Top down, sun bath. One of those drives where you pass stores called Minnie Mae's Attic and Chihuahua Tire Sales. Where you pass a guy bebopping unintelligible on the side of the road, and you envy his offbeat high-hearted rhythm. One of those drives where you laugh and wish for chicken wings and a friend named Weird April.

# Re: F

*A Found Poem Made Up Entirely of Email Subject Lines
All Spam (including the title)*


It's all about Kim.
She's 51 years old, but looks 28.
Creative concealment
purchased with confidence.
Booty call request waiting.
Secret admirer.
Magic Jack,
Handyman available to help you with repairs.
Viagra. Super-Viagra.

61 days.

*Are you caring?
Are you still there?
Sorry to bother you, but is this true?*

Do men always slip away?
Time is running out.

Control the unknown.
Reboot your destiny.
This shouldn't be so hard.

Reboot. Reboot. Reboot.

# Depends on the Day

After breast cancer,
your bra doesn't fit on one side.
That side.
So is your cup half full
or half empty?
You stare in the mirror
and wonder.

# Again

In the middle of a pandemic
a great equalizer
*We're all in this together!*
a white police officer kneels
on the throat of a Black man.
*We can't breathe,* gasp the COVID victims.
*I can't breathe,* gasps the Black man.
They die.
He dies.
Protests. For civic rights. For civil rights.
And we learn again
(Remember Ferguson?) again
(Remember Little Rock?) again
(Remember Greensboro?) again
(Remember Selma to Montgomery?) again
that equality is still a dream
even in a pandemic
*We're (not) all in this together!*
*Hands up! Don't Shoot!*
*I can't breathe . . .*
*I can't breathe . . .*
*I can't breathe . . .*

# Essential

I go to the grocery store to buy essentials
and meet up with a hibiscus instead.
She stands in produce in a forest of trees
braided trunks
bright flowers
buds swelled to burst.
And one with the brightest pink flower
beckons to me near the bananas.
I forget about ground beef, toilet paper,
Clorox wipes, even kitty litter for the cat,
step up to the hibiscus, not caring about
six feet social distancing
hold a limb and say, "You're coming home."
She is essential.

As the numbers climb on the news
so do the number of buds.
The weather roves as wildly as the virus
and I carry the tree in at night to escape frost.
I can protect her. I know I can protect her
as much as I wish I could protect my daughter
my husband
my adult kids, all essential workers.
My granddaughter, whom I can no longer see.
The hibiscus and I stay home.
Neither of us wear masks.
I breathe her in.

As the temperature warms, her buds bloom
one, two, three, four, five.
Four Supreme Court judges decide to throw
Wisconsin's door wide open, even as the
governor stands spread-eagled and wide-armed
in the jamb.
The hibiscus and I stay home
(as the governor suggested)
and I praise her for her beauty and intelligence.
While some run to bars, I drink in her blooms
and we sit together under the sun.
Under the stars.

During the day now, I sit on the deck,
press her leaves together in my palms,
and we pray for what is essential as
my family heads out to work among those
who refuse to wear masks
stand too close
laugh too loud
declare their civic right
to hurt others.
I look at the bright pink flowers, the buds swollen
with the promise of more color to come.
And she reminds me that I am safe
that the world is a beautiful place
that I am doing my absolute best to protect
those I love and those I don't know
And that compassion and kindness
are essential.

## Social Distance

On the day we are told we're
"a national emergency"
two days after the world spins into
"a pandemic"
I leave the gym behind
out of good sense
practicality
trying to stay healthy by leaving
a place that was making me healthy.
I take an evening walk by the Fox River
a Fitbit counting my steps instead
of a treadmill readout.
I see:
Spring's robins
returned geese,
long-lasting ducks,
swans with necks curved in
half a Valentine's heart.
I duck every time I hear a
red-winged blackbird call.
A muskrat swims through
what must still be winter water.
A toppled grandfather tree.
And an empty playground.
I think of 1918
and try hard to see 2020.
Back home, I sit in front of my computer.

See the living lights of Facebook,
Twitter,
Instagram.
Imagine the chatter
and raise my hand to high-five
the screen.

# When a City Screams

*For Waukesha, Wisconsin*
*My home*

*On November 21, 2021, while we were still all in the grip of the pandemic, my city of Waukesha, Wisconsin, decided to hold its annual holiday parade. Partway through the event, Darrell Brooks, while running from the police, crashed his SUV through the parade barricades, and mowed down everyone he could reach. Six people died, sixty-two were injured, and Waukesha was left in shock to start the hard work toward recovery. On November 16, 2022, Brooks was sentenced to six consecutive life sentences without the possibility of parole, plus an additional 762.5 years to be served consecutively.*

When a city screams,
it raises one voice, but many sounds
the shrill cry of the young
the gravel of age
melody of female
harmony of male
dissonance of shock
allegro of fear
and even a gasp of disbelief.
But one voice, one voice
at once.
Together.

I heard my little city scream
on November 21, 2021
at a holiday Christmas parade.
I heard my city's voice
and then its sobs.
I wanted to dry its tears
but I couldn't see through my own.

My voice rose
screamed
sobbed
joined as one
Together

with my little city.

# At the Registration Desk at the Y

Her therapist declared,
"Someone with a death wish
doesn't register for swimming lessons."
So she went to the Y, signed the form,
then smiled and waved before
stepping into the deep end.

# Rhymes

*haiku*

There's a reason why
Suicide and Crucified
rhyme. Killers of souls.

# Fall

When a whale is ready to die,
he sinks to the ocean floor and
lies still until he's gone.
He leaves his body to the rest of
Life in the sea.
Scientists call this Whale Fall.

When a jet is going to crash,
the pilots work through their to-do lists
and try to save the plane
as long as they are airborne.
Until they're not.
The plane falls.

At night, I sink onto my bed and
I lie still.
I look at the ceiling and count the
things on my to-do list, the things I
did today, the things I need to do
tomorrow. I count.
I am calm.
I am airborne.
Until I am not.

Let me Fall.
Just please
let me Fall.
Let the rest of Life
live off of me.
I count.
I am airborne.

# Reality Calling

You know, sometimes praying
is just wishful thinking
and dandelion fluff just doesn't
make for a warm bed.
You can't get a meal from a
turkey wishbone.
And a lucky rabbit's foot just
left the rabbit dead.

# By and By

When she takes off her wedding ring,
lays it gently on their kitchen table
the circle is still unbroken.
But she is shattered.

# Missing on CraigsList's Missed Connections

*a series of haiku*

1.
looking on craigslist's
missed connections for my life
Google didn't have it

2.
looking on craigslist's
missed connections for a man
I made up last night

3.
looking on craigslist's
missed connections for a man
who thinks I am alive

4.
looking on craigslist's
missed connections for myself
I got lost out there

5.
looking on craigslist's
lost and found and there I was
not missing at all.

# My Place

He said I needed to be put back into my place.
My place his definition, of course.
But I am already there.
And it's my definition that matters.
I've worked very hard to get here.
Word by word by word.
There is no "putting back".
There is only moving forward.
And that is what I will do.
Word by word by word.

# When a Man Turns a Cartwheel

When he turns a cartwheel in
the Pacific's sand,
and then he turns another one,
I can tell he pictures his legs straight,
toes to the sun,
back ramrod,
elbows lifting him skyward like a starfish.
But they aren't. He isn't.
When he comes upright, he staggers,
a bit like a drunk on his way home.
He beams at me.
And I applaud.

# The Truth About Cows

I was late in years when I was told the truth,
a truth I should have guessed as a young woman
pregnant with my first child, then my second and my third.
My breasts heavy with baby after baby's milk. Heavy, with
swollen nipples which always had just a drop or two more
from each to stain my clothes.
My friend, another heavy-breasted woman of later years,
who grew up on a dairy farm, compared herself to a cow
as we sat, having tea in the kitchen, and noticed our breasts
resting on the table.
Years after babies.
Years after husbands.
Still resting.
And that's when she told me that cows only give milk when
they are pregnant.
And so they are pregnant. Again and again.
Always.
And when they can't be pregnant,
they're slaughtered.
I didn't know. I guess I thought that Mother Nature was at play,
and that somehow, milk magically streamed from the udders
that swung low and slow between cows' back legs.
Magic milk produced from green grass and yellow hay,
    honeysuckle
and buttercups, fresh creek water and clean clear air, and
    afternoons
standing in the sun.
Resting.
Not so, my friend said. Not so. The cows were kept constantly
    pregnant.

Serviced by a bull. Over and over. The cows tied to hold them still.
The baby girls set aside to raise for more milk, pregnancy after
pregnancy after pregnancy. Bull after bull.
A select few boys kept for more service, but the rest left to lay in
   the field.
Bawling. Until they bawled no more.
I bawled.
Then I went upstairs and stripped to my waist.
In the mirror, I looked at my breasts, my heavy, heavy breasts,
late in years, and I hoisted them up in my hands.
When I dropped them, they swayed low and slow
like an udder.
And I saw the cow that I am.
Years after babies.
Years after husbands.
But still tied to keep me still.
A quart of milk souring in the fridge.

# Retreat

When I stay at the little house
with the ocean in the back yard
I never shut the door to the bathroom.
I soak in the shower 'til the water runs cold.
Only do laundry when I have no more clothes.
Make coffee while standing naked in the kitchen.
Eat what I want when I want.
Breakfast can be at noon
Lunch at four
Dinner deep into the night.
I talk to myself and
talk to the ocean and
talk to the words on my computer screen.
There is an open book on the kitchen table
another book beside the bed
a third by the couch
and I replace them with others when I'm done.
I take walks by myself
sleep by myself.
sit at the computer
and the television
and the deck overlooking the ocean
by myself.
And it's so, so quiet.
But in the middle of the night
when I look out the window from the bed
and I see the light from a passing fishing boat
like a bobbing star on the waves
I am happy for the company.

# God, Adam, Eve, and Woman

They say that Adam was made in God's image, and I believe it, she says, and that God's a man. Because only a man would make a man tall, blond and ripped, with a dick so large, it had to be covered by the leaf of the ficus lyrata to make him modest, and to keep Adam from fiddling with himself.

And true to form, she belly-laughs.

And when Adam whined that he needed to fiddle, and God figured fiddling was sinful (self-abuse), He reached into Adam's stomach (the way to a man is through his stomach) and plucked Himself a rib. Thin and curved. God awarded Adam with boners in exchange for his sacrifice and then God waved His wand (it ain't the size of the wand, remember, but the magic, though I think one can assume God's is both big and magical; he's God, she says) and there was Eve. Born of Adam's rib and God's wand. She was tall, blonde and built, with boobs huge and bare; who cared about modesty there, expose the jugs, and He hid her bush with another leaf. How the hell do you hide a bush with a leaf? If a tree falls in the forest, does it make a sound?

You figure it out, she says.

Well, at least this is what the artists depict, and given our history, it makes sense. Artists are known for the truth. Well, sometimes. Look at David and Venus di Milo. So Eve, by Adam's desire and maybe God's own, didn't have a brain, but she did have an appetite, though it wasn't necessarily for Adam's dick. Eve hungered for something big and red and crunchy, and well, you just don't get that giving head. Much. So Eve was hungry for something she didn't have, and she ate the apple and you know the rest. If it was left to Eve, and Adam, and God, Womanhood would be damned for all eternity.

Funny, she says, that a bone-skinny woman would be cursed for eating something healthy.

But see, then Woman had a taste. She learned Delicious. Woman kept the rib, but began to pack the meat on. Blonde, hungry, little-brain Eve took her appetite and her fig leaf and her jugs and propagated and Amazons cracked out of her eggs. They prowled through the $14^{th}$-century, larger than life, larger than love, larger than an apple, and they grew and they felt their size. They felt their voices. They found their power. They fought in wars. And won.

And yeah, she says, Amazons cut off one breast. The better to fit their weapons. They had to learn to deal with their own roundness. And learn the weapon that was theirs. Then they grew 'em back.

Before the $14^{th}$ century turned to the $15^{th}$, Amazons burst out voluptuous, and the word Voluptuous was born. It meant full of pleasure. Pleasure! she says. Because Men began to grow too and slid their eyes from the Eves of the world and ran their gazes up, down, over, around and under the Amazons. Sized them up. Full of pleasure. Just bursting.

You just gotta bust what's bursting, she says. You just gotta touch.

In the 15th century, Voluptuous was tagged as Addiction. Addiction to "sensual pleasure." Hooked on Fornication! It doesn't take even a brain the size of Eve's to figure what happened there. Men, Women, Amazons, more cushion, less pushin', luxury, lavish, buffet, grab a big breast here, grab a fat ass there, and oh, baby, baby, feel the ground move! Feel it howl and rumble!

And roar! she says.

In the 16th century, Peter Paul Rubens arrived, and so did his ladies in their altogether and folks lined up to stare, she says. Like the cat that ate the canary. Like the man that ate the woman and the woman that ate the man and they ate together out of the raw bounty this world has to offer.

Some said the word Rubenesque like it was a bad taste in their mouths, but some let it roll around their tongues and their teeth and they pooched out their cheeks and you just know there was Feasting going on. Finger-lickin' Feasting with saliva and semen and salty juices galore. In the art studio. Behind the galleries. In rooms everywhere. You can bet these weren't titters from teeny tiny tits, but the raucous from outrageous breadths. Powerful, like Amazons. Appetite, like Eve. And Sensual from one roll to the next on a curvy couch of a body that just sunk Man's ass in. And his dick too, from behind the ficus.

They fiddled, she says, and giggles.

Somehow, in the 30s, the word Zaftig appeared, sounding ominous and Nazi and harsh. Yet it was the Jews that created it, the Jews that erupted it, and it meant juicy and succulent and Woman. Woman! A Zaftig Woman was a Rubenesque Woman, an Amazon of fulfilling desires. And Voluptuous cavorted with Webster the Second and birthed sensual pleasure and feminine beauty combined. Connected. One.

Feminine beauty, she says. And places a hand gently on her bust.

So a Voluptuous Woman is a beautiful Woman. And a Voluptuous Woman is a Zaftig Woman. And a Zaftig Woman is a Rubenesque Woman. And a Rubinesque Woman is an Amazon, borne straight out of Eve's slender thighs. We've come a long way since an apple in the garden.

A long way since God and His image, she says.

Did God create us? Not even close. He made a Xerox of His image and then Eve from a rib bone for Man and his ficus lyrata. Woman made Woman, hungering hard from Eve's appetite and forming bodies thick with our souls. With our voices and our strengths and our desires.

God and His image be damned. It took a Fat Girl to set this world straight, she says. Hallelujah. And Amen.

# About the Author

Kathie Giorgio is the critically acclaimed author of eight novels, two story collections, a collection of essays, and four poetry books. She's been nominated for the Pushcart Prize in fiction and poetry and awarded the Outstanding Achievement Award from the Wisconsin Library Association, the Silver Pen Award for Literary Excellence, the Pencraft Award for Literary Excellence, and the Eric Hoffer Award in Fiction.

Her poem "Light" won runner-up in the 2021 *Rosebud Magazine* Poetry Prize, and her poem "Again" won first prize in the Wisconsin Writers Association's Jade Ring contest. She is a two-time runner-up of the Zona Gale Short Fiction Award for her stories "Quiet" and "Recipe." Her short story, "Snapdragon" was performed for the Stories on Stage series at Su Teatro theatre in Boulder, Colorado. Her poem "Harvest Moon" was included in the Poetry Leaves exhibition in Waterford, Michigan. In a recent column, Jim Higgins, the books editor of the *Milwaukee Journal Sentinel,* included Giorgio's short story collection *Enlarged Hearts* on a list of the top 21 books by Wisconsin writers of the 21$^{st}$ century.

Besides being a writer, Giorgio is the director and founder of the international creative writing studio AllWriters' Workplace & Workshop LLC. AllWriters' offers online and onsite courses and workshops in all genres and abilities of creative writing, as well as coaching and editing services. Thousands of writers worldwide have gotten their start at AllWriters', and thousands have continued their career there. Giorgio has taught for 30 years.

Giorgio lives in Waukesha, Wisconsin. Three of her adult children, Christopher, Andy, and Olivia, live close by, along with her solo granddaughter, Maya Mae. One adult child, Katie, has wandered off to Louisiana where she teaches at the University of Louisiana—Lafayette and lives among the mathematicians and alligators.

Kathie's website:
kathiegiorgio.org

AllWriters' Workplace & Workshop LLC:
allwritersworkshop.com.

www.ingramcontent.com/pod-product-compliance
Lightning Source LLC
Chambersburg PA
CBHW030911170426
43193CB00009BA/817